ACCOUNTING LIFEPAC 4
POSTING TO THE GENERAL LEDGER

CONTENTS

Author: Daniel L. Ritzman, B.S.
Editors: Alan Christopherson, M.S.
                 Jennifer L. Davis, B.S.

Alpha Omega Publications®

804 N. 2nd Ave. E., Rock Rapids, IA 51246-1759

© MM by Alpha Omega Publications, Inc.   All rights reserved.

LIFEPAC is a registered trademark of Alpha Omega Publications, Inc.

ACCOUNTING LIFEPAC 4
POSTING TO THE GENERAL LEDGER

OVERVIEW

This LIFEPAC® will take you through the third step in the financial process: posting. Step one is to analyze each transaction to see what accounts are affected. The second step is to record the debit and credit parts of each transaction, listing the accounts that are changed as a result of the transaction. This information is recorded in the general journal. In step three the transactions in the general journal are posted to individual accounts which are grouped together in the general ledger. The ledger sorts by account the transactions recorded in the journal and provides a quick summary of the activity that has occurred in each of the accounts. You will also learn how to determine ledger account balances and prove the accuracy of your posting by preparing a trial balance.

OBJECTIVES

When you have completed this LIFEPAC you will be able to:

1. Define accounting terms associated with posting transactions from the general journal to the general ledger.

2. Identify accounting concepts.

3. Explain the purpose and use of a chart of accounts.

4. Prepare a chart of accounts based on the balance sheet and income statement.

5. Accurately post from a general journal to a general ledger.

6. Prepare a cash proof.

7. Prepare a trial balance.

VOCABULARY

Account – a device used to summarize all the changes that affect a single item in the accounting equation.

Account Balance – the difference between the debits and credits recorded in an account.

Account Number – the number assigned to an account in the ledger.

Balance Column Account – an account that has debit and credit columns for entering changes in the account and a column for entering the new account balance after each debit or credit is posted to the account.

Balance Sheet – a form that shows the financial position of a business on a specific date.

Book of Original Entry – a journal in which transactions are first recorded.

Book of Secondary Entry – a ledger to which amounts from the journal are posted.

Chart of Accounts – a list of all the accounts used by a business entity.

File Maintenance – the procedure of arranging accounts in a general ledger, inserting and deleting accounts, and keeping records current.

General Ledger – a book that contains all of the accounts needed to prepare the financial reports of a business entity.

Income Statement – a financial statement that reports the revenue, expenses, and net income or net loss of a business for a specific period of time.

Ledger – a group of accounts.

Opening an Account – writing the account title and number on the heading line of an account.

Opening Entry – the first entry made in a general journal that opens the accounts in a new set of books.

Posting – transferring information from a journal entry to a ledger account.

Proving Cash – the process of determining whether the amount of cash, both on hand and in the bank, is the same amount that exists in the accounting records.

Trial Balance – a proof (test) to show that the total debit balances in the ledger equal the total credit balances.

SECTION I. THE LEDGER ACCOUNTS

Most small businesses record transactions in a general journal. A journal is a record of the debit and credit parts of each business transaction. These transactions are entered (journalized) in chronological order. The journal is referred to as the **book of original entry**. If the journal was the only tool used in the accounting system of a business, the bookkeeper would have to sort through all the journal pages to find any entry affecting a single account in the system. In order to determine the account balance the bookkeeper would have to go through every journal entry and make a list of all debit and credit entries to that account. This would be very-time consuming, and the accuracy of the work would be in question.

For this reason, accountants designed a form called an **account** that summarizes in one place all the changes to a single item on the chart of accounts. Each item in the accounting system has its own account, and these individual accounts are collected into a book called a **ledger**. The ledger is called the **book of secondary entry**.

Every entry in the general journal is transferred to the ledger accounts in a procedure called **posting**. Posting is the third step in the financial process.

Types of Ledger Accounts

Each ledger account has a debit and credit side just like the T accounts you used in LIFEPAC 3. Like a general journal, it also has space to record the transaction date and the journal page number (the source of the transaction). You will find this information helpful in tracing a specific entry back to the journal where it originated.

Two-Column Ledger Account. One type of a general ledger account called the two-column ledger is illustrated below, along with its relationship to the T account.

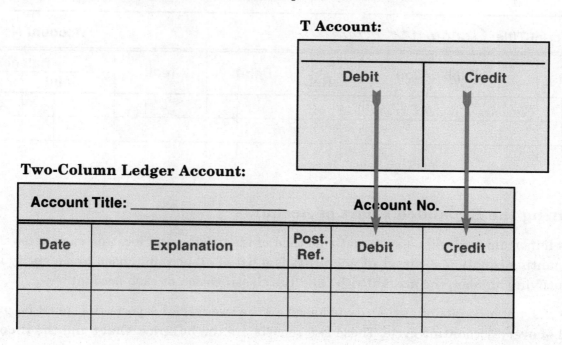

A disadvantage of this account form is that no current account balance is shown. The bookkeeper must determine the current balance each time the account is used. This procedure is difficult and time-consuming if the account has a large number of entries; therefore, it is advantageous to use a four-column account called a **balance column ledger account**.

Balance Column Ledger Account. This type of account allows for a running balance of each account to be calculated at all times. Like the two-column account form, the balance-column account has debit and credit columns for entering changes in the account. In addition, it has a debit balance or credit balance column for entering the new debit or credit balance after each transaction is posted. This balance column account form is illustrated below.

Balance Column Ledger Account:

Account Title:							Account No.	
Date	Explanation	Post. Ref.	Debit		Credit		Balance	
							Debit	Credit

To use the balance column account effectively, the balance must be entered on the first line of the ledger account. Usually, only the permanent accounts (assets, liabilities, and owner's equity) have balances for the beginning of a fiscal period. The temporary accounts (revenue and expenses) are normally closed at the end of a fiscal period and have no balances to carry forward.

When the ledger page becomes full, the balance needs to be transferred to a new ledger page. In the example below, the date and the words "Balance Brought Forward," plus the last balance from the previous ledger page, are written in the balance column of the next page for that ledger account. A check mark (✔) is placed in the Post. Ref. column to indicate that this amount was carried forward rather than being posted from a journal entry.

Account Title: *Accounts Payable*							Account No. *210*	
Date 20—	Explanation	Post. Ref.	Debit		Credit		Balance	
							Debit	Credit
Jan. 1	Balance Brought Forward	✔						6150 00

Preparing the Expanded Chart of Accounts

It is important to design a systematic method of identifying and locating each account used in the accounting equation. A **chart of accounts** is a list of all accounts used by an entity indicating the identifying number, the account title, and the classification of each account.

The chart of accounts of any entity is based on the two formal reports that must be prepared at the end of every accounting cycle. These two reports are the **balance sheet** and the **income statement**.

In LIFEPAC 2 you learned how to prepare a partial chart of accounts that included only the balance sheet items: assets, liabilities and capital. This LIFEPAC will discuss how to create an expanded chart of accounts that includes income statement items: revenue and expenses.

As you studied in LIFEPAC 2, the design of a numbering system should provide adequate flexibility to permit expansion without having to revise the basic system. Generally, blocks of numbers are assigned to various groups of accounts such as assets, liabilities, capital, revenue and expenses. The numbering system must commonly consist of three or four digits. The setup of a numbering system is usually at the discretion of the accountant.

An example of a system designed for a service business might appear as follows:

Assets accounts	110 through 199
Liability accounts	210 through 299
Capital accounts	310 through 399
Revenue accounts	410 through 499
Expense accounts	510 through 599

The first digit indicates the classification of the account, and the second or third number indicates the position of that account in the category.

Shown below is an expanded chart of accounts for **Kline's Cleaning Service**, owned by Art Kline.

KLINE'S CLEANING SERVICE CHART OF ACCOUNTS			
Balance Sheet Accounts		**Income Statement Accounts**	
Assets		**Revenue**	
Cash	110	Sales	410
Petty Cash	120	**Expenses**	
Supplies	130	Advertising Expense	510
Prepaid Insurance	140	Miscellaneous Expense	520
Equipment	150	Rent Expense	530
Liabilities		Repair Expense	540
Main's Supply Co.	210	Supplies Expense	550
Office Max	220	Utilities Expense	560
Mike's Garage	230		
Owner's Equity			
Art Kline, Capital	310		
Art Kline, Drawing	320		

The general ledger accounts are numbered in the order in which they appear on the balance sheet and income statement. This system organizes the ledger in such a manner that the accounts with common characteristics are grouped together:

1. Assets are listed in order of liquidity. Liquidity is the ease in which the assets account can be converted to cash.

2. Liabilities are listed in alphabetical order.

3. Owner's Equity is listed by investment (Capital) and withdrawals (Drawing).

4. Revenue and expense accounts are usually listed in alphabetical order.

The accounts are numbered using increments of ten. This allows flexibility to add accounts without revising the entire numbering system.

A general ledger is usually assembled in a loose-leaf binder which permits insertion and deletion of pages without handicapping the system. This also allows new accounts to be added between existing accounts, with a new number assigned between the existing numbers in the system. In this way, all accounts with the same characteristics remain in the same position of the ledger.

The general ledger binder is assembled so that assets are placed first, liability accounts are second, owner's equity is third, revenue is fourth, and expenses are fifth. This matches the development of the numbering system used on the chart of accounts. A binder compiled in this manner leads to consistency between the chart of accounts, analyzing transactions, journalizing, posting to the general ledger, and the system of financial reporting.

Accountants remove accounts that are no longer needed and assign the existing number to a new account with the same classification. They also will divide accounts that are currently in use. If a business is using just one revenue account, Sales (410), but it is discovered that a greater proportion of revenue than expected is being received from vending machines, then the accountant will set up two revenue accounts: one for Sales (410) and the other for Vending Machine Income (420), thus presenting a more accurate picture of revenue sources.

With the current numbering system, this new account can be added at the end of the list because in the example Sales (410) comes alphabetically before Vending Machine Income (420).

Another example of the flexibility of this type of numbering system would be the insertion of Delivery Expense between Advertising Expense (510) and Insurance Expense (520). In this example, Delivery Expense would be assigned 515 to keep the expense in the proper order. The process of arranging the general ledger, inserting and deleting accounts, and keeping records current is called **file maintenance**.

 Review the material in this section in preparation for the Self Test. The Self Test will check your mastery of this particular section. The items missed on this Self Test will indicate specific areas where restudy is needed for mastery.

SELF TEST 1

Answer these questions (each answer, 5 points).

1.01 Which two financial statements are the basis for the expanded chart of accounts?

    a. _____

    b. _____

1.02 What is the main advantage of the balance-column ledger account?

_____

_____

_____

Define the following terms (each answer, 10 points).

1.03 Account: _____

_____

_____

1.04 General ledger: _____

_____

_____

1.05 Chart of accounts: _____

_____

_____

1.06 File maintenance: _____

_____

_____

Complete these activities (each lettered answer, 3 points).

1.07 List the five divisions of an expanded chart of accounts and the number for each division:

Division	Number
a. _____	_____
b. _____	_____
c. _____	_____
d. _____	_____
e. _____	_____

1.08 Organize the following accounts in the order they would appear on the chart of accounts, then assign each a number according to the current numbering system:

Cash • Jennie Johnson, Capital • Advertising Expense • Sales
Accounts Payable • Miscellaneous Expense • Supplies

Account Title	*Account Number*
a. _____	_____
b. _____	_____
c. _____	_____
d. _____	_____
e. _____	_____
f. _____	_____
g. _____	_____

Score _____

Adult Check _____

Initial   Date

SECTION II: THE POSTING PROCEDURE

Opening the Ledger

The procedure of writing an account title and account number on the heading of an account form is called **opening an account**. A ledger account must be opened for each item listed on the chart of accounts. The general ledger accounts are numbered and arranged in the same order as they appear on the chart of accounts. All of the general ledger accounts listed on the chart of accounts must be opened using the same procedure.

Account Title: *Cash*					Account No. *110*	
Date	Explanation	Post. Ref.	Debit	Credit	Balance	
					Debit	Credit

Since each account will contain several business transactions, using the balance account form provides a current balance for each transaction posted. It becomes necessary to write the account name and number again only when a ledger page is filled and the balance is carried forward to a new page, as discussed in Section I of this LIFEPAC.

Posting Journal Entries to the Ledger

The process of transferring information from the journal to the ledger is known as **posting**. Once a journal entry has been recorded in the journal, it needs to be posted to the appropriate ledger accounts. The posting process sorts each journal entry so that all debits and credits affecting each account are brought together in one place. For example, all changes to cash are brought together in the cash account.

The frequency of posting can vary from business to business. With the invention of the automated accounting system, posting from the journal to the ledger is accomplished automatically as items are journalized and new balances are calculated immediately. When posting manually, the journal entries may be posted at the end of each day or even at the end of a week or month, depending on the number of transactions.

Large businesses must post daily to keep their records up to date. Smaller businesses may be able to vary posting frequency according to the volume of business.

Even though the frequency of posting varies, the procedure remains the same. Most accountants suggest that all the transactions for one day be posted at the end of that day. This makes finding and correcting errors much easier—each transaction for that day is easier to remember and easier to trace. It will also reduce the amount of time spent posting.

As in the journalizing process, posting is completed from the left of the account form to the right. In the posting procedure, any journal debit becomes a ledger account debit and any journal credit becomes a ledger account credit. All amounts entered in the general journal must be posted to the accounts in the ledger. By making sure all items are posted accurately, it is easier to summarize the results. In order for the ledger to become a reliable source of information for preparing financial statements, accurate posting procedures must be maintained for the entire accounting period.

In LIFEPAC 2 you learned how to record and post the opening journal entry. An opening entry opens the accounts in a new set of books. The source document for the opening entry is the beginning balance sheet for the new business. The amounts posted to the ledger accounts in the opening entry represent the value of those accounts at the opening of the business.

Once the opening entry has been recorded and posted and the permanent ledger accounts are established, the day-to-day business operations are then recorded in the journal, as you learned in LIFEPAC 3. Those transactions are also posted to the ledger accounts. The posting procedure for the daily transactions of a business is described below.

Posting Procedure. To post a journal entry to the ledger accounts, follow these steps.

Post the **debit** parts:

1. Enter the **date of the journal entry** in the date column of the ledger account (see the example on the next page).
2. Enter the **journal page number** in the Post. Ref. column of the account.
3. Enter the **amount of the debit** in the debit amount column of the appropriate ledger account.
4. Add the amount to the previous debit balance (if any) and enter the new balance in the debit balance column.
5. **Return to the journal and enter the ledger account number** in the Post. Ref. column. This indicates to which account the amount was posted.

Post the **credit** parts:

6. Enter the **date of the journal entry** in the date column of the ledger account (see the example on the next page).
7. Enter the **journal page number** in the Post. Ref. column of the account.
8. Enter the **amount of the credit** in the credit amount column of the appropriate ledger account.
9. Add the amount to the previous credit balance (if any) and enter the new balance in the credit balance column.
10. **Return to the journal** (shown below) **and enter the ledger account number** in the Post. Ref. column. This indicates to which account the amount was posted.

Date 20—	Account Title and Explanation	Doc No.	Post. Ref.	General Debit		General Credit	
Jan. 1	Cash	5	110	15000	00		
	Art Kline, Capital	M1	310	**10**		15000	00

JOURNAL — Page 1

Account Title: Cash   **Account No.** 110

Date 20—		Explanation	Post. Ref.	Debit		Credit		Balance Debit		Balance Credit	
Jan. 1			J1	15000	00			15000	00		
1			**2**	**3**				**4**			

Account Title: Art Kline, Capital   **Account No.** 310

Date 20—		Explanation	Post. Ref.	Debit		Credit		Balance Debit		Balance Credit	
Jan. 1			J1			15000	00			15000	00
6			**7**			**8**				**9**	

Determining the Account Balance

The type of balance an account has (debit or credit) corresponds to the position of that account in the accounting equation.

Type of Account	Normal Balance	Increase Side	Decrease Side
Asset Accounts	Debit Balance	Debit	Credit
Liability Accounts	Credit Balance	Credit	Debit
Capital Accounts	Credit Balance	Credit	Debit
Revenue Accounts	Credit Balance	Credit	Debit
Expense Accounts	Debit Balance	Debit	Credit

Posting Credits to Accounts with Debit Balances. Shown below is what happens to the normal debit balance of an asset account (Cash) when a credit amount (paying $500.00 for supplies, for example) is posted. The transaction creates a credit to the cash account. Cash is an asset. Asset accounts increase on the debit side and decrease on the credit side. Therefore, you would subtract the credit of $500.00 from a current balance of $3,500.00 and bring forward the new balance of $3,000.00.

Account Title: Cash   **Account No.** 110

Date 20—		Explanation	Post. Ref.	Debit		Credit		Balance Debit		Balance Credit	
Aug. 2			J1	3500	00			3500	00		
	5		J1			500	00	3000	00		

11

Posting Debits to Accounts with Credit Balances. Shown below is what happens to the normal credit balance of a liability account (Accounts Payable) when a debit amount (paying $3,000.00 on account) is posted. The transaction creates a debit to the liability account. Accounts Payable is a liability. Liability accounts increase on the credit side and decrease on the debit side. Therefore, you would subtract the debit of $3,000.00 from a current balance of $3,000.00 and bring forward the new balance of zero. In this illustration, the balance was reduced to zero because the entire liability was paid. A line is drawn across the balance column to indicate that the account has been zeroed out; that is, the entire balance was paid and the new account balance is zero.

Account Title: *Accounts Payable*					Account No. *210*		
Date 20—	Explanation	Post. Ref.	Debit	Credit	Balance		
					Debit	Credit	
Jan. 1		*J1*		*3000 00*		*3000*	*00*
2		*J1*	*3000 00*			——	

Complete this activity.

2.1 Post the remainder of the journal entries for **Kline's Cleaning Service** on the next page to the appropriate accounts. The ledger accounts have already been opened for you and the first transaction has been posted as an example. NOTE: Be sure to bring the new balance forward. Remember the following accounting rules about debits and credits:

ASSETS:	LIABILITIES:	CAPITAL:
debits increase	credits increase	credits increase
credits decrease	debits decrease	debits decrease

JOURNAL

Date 20—		Account Title and Explanation	Doc No.	Post. Ref.	General Debit		General Credit	
Jan.	1	Cash		110	15000	00		
		Art Kline, Capital	M1	310			15000	00
	2	Cash			1500	00		
		Sales	I12				1500	00
	5	Advertising Expense			150	00		
		Cash	Ck 3				150	00
	6	Accounts Payable			6150	00		
		Cash	Ck 4				6150	00
	12	Cash			1000	00		
		Sales	I13				1000	00
	16	Art Kline, Drawing			600	00		
		Cash	Ck 5				600	00

Account Title: Cash **Account No.** 110

Date 20—		Explanation	Post. Ref.	Debit		Credit		Balance Debit		Balance Credit	
Jan.	1		J1	15000	00			15000	00		

Account Title: Accounts Payable **Account No.** 210

Date 20—	Explanation	Post. Ref.	Debit		Credit		Balance Debit		Balance Credit	
Jan.	Balance Brought Forward	✔							6150	00

Account Title: *Art Kline, Capital*   **Account No.** *310*

Date 20—		Explanation	Post. Ref.	Debit		Credit		Balance Debit		Credit	
Jan.	1		J1			15000	00			15000	00

Account Title: *Art Kline, Drawing*   **Account No.** *320*

Date 20—		Explanation	Post. Ref.	Debit		Credit		Balance Debit		Credit	

Account Title: *Sales*   **Account No.** *410*

Date 20—		Explanation	Post. Ref.	Debit		Credit		Balance Debit		Credit	

Account Title: *Advertising Expense*   **Account No.** *510*

Date 20—		Explanation	Post. Ref.	Debit		Credit		Balance Debit		Credit	

Proving the Cash Account

When cash is received and paid out, the transactions are recorded in the journal and then posted to the Cash account in the ledger. If all payments are made by check and all cash receipts are deposited in the checking account, the balance of the checkbook and the balance of the ledger account should both be the same.

Proving cash is the process of determining whether the amount of cash, both on hand and in the bank, is the same amount that exists in the accounting records. Cash should be proved at least once a month. Many small businesses find it to their advantage to prove cash once a week. On the other hand, most retail stores prove cash daily because of the large volume of money they handle on any given day.

Ledger Account:

Date 20—		Explanation	Post. Ref.	Debit		Credit		Balance Debit		Balance Credit	
Jan.	1		J1	15000	00			15000	00		
	2		J1	1500	00			16500	00		
	5		J1			150	00	16350	00		
	6		J1			6150	00	10200	00		
	12		J1	1000	00			11200	00		
	16		J1			600	00	10600	00		

Account Title: *Cash*   Account No. 110

Checkbook:

Check No.	16
Date	, 20___
To	
For	
Balance Forwarded	10600 00
Deposit	

Steps to prove cash:

1. Determine the ledger account balance by finding the last balance entered in the debit column of the cash account.

2. Determine the checkbook balance by finding the balance brought forward on the last check stub.

3. Compare the checkbook balance with the cash account balance.

4. When both figures agree, cash has been proved.

Complete these activities.

Buford Burke owns a shop called **Burke's Bagels**. The beginning balance sheet for the shop is shown below, along with a memo with instructions from the owner.

Burke's Bagels
Balance Sheet
June 1, 20–

Assets			Liabilities		
Cash	1400	00	Accounts Payable 1100.00		
Accounts Receivable	600	00	Notes Payable 700.00		
Supplies	1400	00	Total Liabilities	1800	00
Prepaid Insurance	500	00			
Equipment	2600	00	Capital		
			Buford Burke, Capital	4700	00
Total Assets	6500	00	Total Liabilities & Capital	6500	00

B̦B̦   Burke's Bagels   No. 1

Please record the opening entry. For account information, use the beginning balance sheet (attached) dated June 1, 20__ .

Buford B. Burke
January 1, 20__ .

2.2   **Open the ledger**, using the following account titles and numbers:

Cash	110	Accounts Payable	210
Accounts Receivable	120	Notes Payable	220
Supplies	130	Buford Burke, Capital	310
Prepaid Insurance	140	Buford Burke, Drawing	320
Equipment	150	Sales	410
		Rent Expense	510

2.3   **Record the opening entry** in the journal for **Burke's Bagels**, using the information shown on the balance sheet.

2.4   **Post the opening entry** to the ledger.

16

JOURNAL

Date	Account Title and Explanation	Doc No.	Post. Ref.	General Debit		General Credit	

Account Title:					Account No.		
Date	Explanation	Post. Ref.	Debit	Credit	Balance		
					Debit	Credit	

Account Title:					Account No.		
Date	Explanation	Post. Ref.	Debit	Credit	Balance		
					Debit	Credit	

Account Title:					Account No.		
Date	Explanation	Post. Ref.	Debit	Credit	Balance		
					Debit	Credit	

Account Title:					Account No.		
Date	Explanation	Post. Ref.	Debit	Credit	Balance		
					Debit	Credit	

Account Title:						Account No.		
Date	Explanation	Post. Ref.	Debit	Credit	Balance			
					Debit		Credit	

Account Title:						Account No.		
Date	Explanation	Post. Ref.	Debit	Credit	Balance			
					Debit		Credit	

Account Title:						Account No.		
Date	Explanation	Post. Ref.	Debit	Credit	Balance			
					Debit		Credit	

Account Title:						Account No.		
Date	Explanation	Post. Ref.	Debit	Credit	Balance			
					Debit		Credit	

Account Title:						Account No.		
Date	Explanation	Post. Ref.	Debit	Credit	Balance			
					Debit		Credit	

Account Title:						Account No.		
Date	Explanation	Post. Ref.	Debit	Credit	Balance			
					Debit		Credit	

Account Title:							Account No.	
Date	Explanation	Post. Ref.	Debit	Credit	Balance			
					Debit		Credit	

2.5   **Journalize and post** the rest of the transactions for **Burke's Bagels**. If necessary, review the steps for posting found at the beginning of this section.

June   5   Received cash from owner as additional investment $1,500.00, R2

        6   Paid cash for insurance, $150.00, Ck1

        8   Paid cash for supplies, $75.00, Ck2

      10   Bought equipment on account, $100.00, P2

      10   Received cash from sales, $890.00, T2

      12   Paid cash on account, $125.00, Ck3

      13   Paid cash towards loan (Notes Payable), $150.00, Ck4

      17   Received cash from sales, $1,625.00, T3

      19   Paid cash for rent, $350.00, Ck5

      22   Paid cash to owner for personal use, $600.00, Ck6

      23   Received cash on account from a customer, $200.00, R3

2.6   **Prove cash**, using the total of the Cash account and the checkbook balance shown on the check stub below.

         Cash Account Balance: a. _____

         Checkbook Balance: b. _____

Check No. 7		
Date , 20___		
To		
For		
Balance Forwarded	4165	00
Deposit		

 Review the material in this section in preparation for the Self Test. This Self Test will check your mastery of this particular section as well as your knowledge of the previous section.

SELF TEST 2

Match each numbered account from Kline's Cleaning Service with the correct description (each answer, 2 points).

2.01 _____ Advertising Expense (510)

2.02 _____ Sales (410)

2.03 _____ Art Kline, Drawing (320)

2.04 _____ Prepaid Insurance (140)

2.05 _____ Office Max (220)

2.06 _____ Main's Supply Co. (210)

2.07 _____ Cash (110)

2.08 _____ Art Kline, Capital (310)

2.09 _____ Supplies (130)

2.010 _____ Utilities Expense (560)

2.011 _____ Equipment (150)

2.012 _____ Petty Cash (120)

a. Asset section, second account

b. Capital section, first account

c. Liability section, second account

d. Asset section, fourth account

e. Expense section, first account

f. Asset section, first account

g. Capital section, second account

h. Liability section, first account

i. Revenue section, first account

j. Asset section, third account

k. Liability section, third account

l. Asset section, fifth account

m. Expense section, sixth account

Number the following steps in the posting procedure in the correct order (each answer, 2 points).

2.013 _____ Write the journal page number in the Post. Ref. column of the account.

2.014 _____ Calculate the new account balance. Enter the new balance in the debit or credit balance column as determined by the account's normal balance.

2.015 _____ Write the account number in the Post. Ref. column of the journal showing the account to which the item was posted.

2.016 _____ Write the date in the date column.

2.017 _____ Write the amount in the debit or credit column of the proper account.

Fill in the blanks with *debit* **or** *credit* (each answer, 2 points).

	Balance Side	Increase Side	Decrease Side
2.018 Asset Accounts	_____	_____	_____
2.019 Liability Accounts	_____	_____	_____
2.020 Capital Accounts	_____	_____	_____
2.021 Revenue Accounts	_____	_____	_____
2.022 Expense Accounts	_____	_____	_____

21

Match the following accounting terms with their definitions (each answer, 2 points).

2.023 _____ a group of accounts

2.024 _____ transferring information from
a journal entry to the ledger account

2.025 _____ a list of all the accounts used by a
business entity

2.026 _____ the first entry made in a general
journal that opens the accounts
in a new set of books

2.027 _____ shows the financial position of a
business on a specific date

2.028 _____ a journal in which transactions
are first recorded

2.029 _____ summarizes all the changes that
affect a single item in the
accounting equation

2.030 _____ arranging accounts in a general ledger
and keeping accounts current

a. posting

b. opening entry

c. chart of accounts

d. book of original entry

e. balance sheet

f. account

g. file maintenance

h. ledger

i. book of secondary entry

j. assets

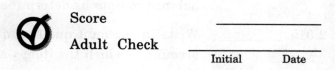

Score _____

Adult Check _____

Initial   Date

SECTION III. PROVING THE LEDGER

Preparing a Trial Balance

When using a double-entry accounting system, debits and credits must always equal each other. A **trial balance** is a proof (test) to show that the total debit balances in the ledger equal the total credit balances. When you prepare a trial balance, you are *proving* that the ledger accounts are in balance.

A trial balance is usually prepared once a month, but it can be prepared at any time during the accounting process, providing that journal entries and posting are current for the time specified. The more times a trial balance is prepared, the more accurate the accounting.

In addition to proving that the debits and credits are in balance, a trial balance also summarizes the balance of each account in the ledger. The accounts are sorted in the same sequence that appears on the chart of accounts: assets first, then liabilities and capital, followed by revenue and expenses. A trial balance is shown below:

1

Joe Blow's Duct Cleaning Service
Trial Balance
September 30, 20—

ACCOUNT TITLE	ACCT. NO.	DEBIT		CREDIT	
Cash	110	5000	00		
Accounts Receivable	120	1000	00		
Prepaid Insurance	130	400	00		
Office Supplies	140	100	00		
Accounts Payable	210			400	00
Joseph Blow, Capital	310			5000	00
Sales	410			2000	00
Advertising Expense	510	50	00		
Rent Expense	520	850	00		
Totals		7400	00	7400	00

1. Prepare the heading the same as you would for a balance sheet with the name of the business, the title of the report, and the date of the report (who, what, when). The date used should be the last date than any transactions were posted in the ledger.

2. The ledger account titles are listed in order with their account numbers. Some accountants prefer to list all accounts whether or not they have balances to ensure that they have not missed an account.

3. The current account balances are entered in the appropriate debit or credit columns.

4. Add the columns and enter the totals, placing a single line across the amount column above the totals and a double line below the totals if they are in balance.

23

Errors in the Trial Balance. Great care must be taken when recording and posting journal entries. Since a trial balance is a good test of the accuracy of posting to a ledger, it is also one of the first places that will reveal errors.

Some common errors revealed by a trial balance include:

1. **Posting to the wrong side of an account**; posting one of the amounts as a debit rather than a credit or vice-versa.

2. **Making a mathematical error** when bringing forward the account balance.

3. **Transposing numbers** when posting an amount; for example, writing $4530.00 when the correct amount is $4350.00.

4. **Posting only half of a transaction**; for example, posting a debit to Cash but forgetting to post the credit to Sales. This type of error is easily avoided if you make sure to record the account numbers in the journal's Post. Ref. column after posting to the ledger account. A quick glance at the Post. Ref. column will tell you if the amounts were posted to both accounts.

However, a trial balance that is in balance—debit amounts equal credit amounts—proves only that the dollar amount of debit balance accounts equals the dollar amount of credit balance accounts. There are certain types of errors that will **not** affect the equality of debits and credits.

1. **Posting to the wrong accounts.** The debits and credits will still balance.

2. **Posting the wrong amounts to the correct accounts.** The debits and credits will still balance.

3. **Omitting an entire transaction.** The omitted transaction will not change debit and credit balances.

4. **Posting the same transaction twice.** The debits and credits are still equal.

Procedure for Searching for Errors:

1. **Re-add** the trial balance columns.

2. **Make sure no accounts have been omitted.** Compare account titles and balances with the general ledger account titles and balances.

3. **Re-add each ledger account** to determine the accuracy of its balance.

4. **Check the posting** of each item from the journal to the ledger. Make sure each posting went to the correct account and no numbers were transposed.

5. **Check the equality** of the debit and credit in the journal.

Complete the following activity.

3.1   **Post the following journal entries for Kline's Cleaning Service**, making sure to bring forward the new account balance after each posting.

Date 20—	Account Title and Explanation	Doc No.	Post. Ref.	General Debit		General Credit	
JOURNAL						Page	1
Jan. 1	Cash			15000	00		
	Art Kline, Capital	M1				15000	00
1	Supplies			6150	00		
	Main's Supply Co.	P2				6150	00
2	Cash			1500	00		
	Sales	I2				1500	00
3	Equipment			8110	00		
	Office Max	P3				8110	00
3	Rent Expense			950	00		
	Cash	Ck 1				950	00
5	Petty Cash			200	00		
	Cash	Ck 2				200	00
5	Cash			1000	00		
	Sales	I5				1000	00
11	Miscellaneous Expense			55	00		
	Cash	Ck 3				55	00
11	Repair Expense			890	00		
	Mike's Garage	M4				890	00
14	Advertising Expense			150	00		
	Cash	Ck 4				150	00
15	Miscellaneous Expense			80	00		
	Cash	Ck 5				80	00
15	Main's Supply Co.			6150	00		
	Cash	Ck 6				6150	00
17	Utilities Expense			980	00		
	Cash	Ck 7				980	00

Date 20—		Account Title and Explanation	Doc No.	Post. Ref.	General Debit		General Credit	
Jan.	18	Cash			2500	00		
		Sales	I18				2500	00
	18	Office Max			2000	00		
		Cash	Ck 8				2000	00
	19	Prepaid Insurance			1150	00		
		Cash	Ck 9				1150	00
	20	Art Kline, Drawing			1500	00		
		Cash	Ck 10				1500	00

Account Title: Cash **Account No.** 110

Date 20—	Explanation	Post. Ref.	Debit	Credit	Balance Debit	Balance Credit

Account Title: *Petty Cash*   Account No. 120

Date 20—		Explanation	Post. Ref.	Debit	Credit	Balance Debit	Balance Credit

Account Title: *Supplies*   Account No. 130

Date 20—		Explanation	Post. Ref.	Debit	Credit	Balance Debit	Balance Credit

Account Title: *Prepaid Insurance*   Account No. 140

Date 20—		Explanation	Post. Ref.	Debit	Credit	Balance Debit	Balance Credit

Account Title: *Equipment*   Account No. 150

Date 20—		Explanation	Post. Ref.	Debit	Credit	Balance Debit	Balance Credit

Account Title: *Main's Supply Co.*   Account No. 210

Date 20—		Explanation	Post. Ref.	Debit	Credit	Balance Debit	Balance Credit

Account Title: Office Max   Account No. 220

Date 20—	Explanation	Post. Ref.	Debit	Credit	Balance Debit	Balance Credit

Account Title: Mike's Garage   Account No. 230

Date 20—	Explanation	Post. Ref.	Debit	Credit	Balance Debit	Balance Credit

Account Title: Art Kline, Capital   Account No. 310

Date 20—	Explanation	Post. Ref.	Debit	Credit	Balance Debit	Balance Credit

Account Title: Art Kline, Drawing   Account No. 320

Date 20—	Explanation	Post. Ref.	Debit	Credit	Balance Debit	Balance Credit

Account Title: Sales   Account No. 410

Date 20—	Explanation	Post. Ref.	Debit	Credit	Balance Debit	Balance Credit

Account Title: Advertising Expense — Account No. 510

Date 20—	Explanation	Post. Ref.	Debit	Credit	Balance Debit	Balance Credit

Account Title: Miscellaneous Expense — Account No. 520

Date 20—	Explanation	Post. Ref.	Debit	Credit	Balance Debit	Balance Credit

Account Title: Rent Expense — Account No. 530

Date 20—	Explanation	Post. Ref.	Debit	Credit	Balance Debit	Balance Credit

Account Title: Repair Expense — Account No. 540

Date 20—	Explanation	Post. Ref.	Debit	Credit	Balance Debit	Balance Credit

Account Title: Supplies Expense — Account No. 550

Date 20—	Explanation	Post. Ref.	Debit	Credit	Balance Debit	Balance Credit

Account Title: _Utilities Expense_						Account No. 560		
Date 20—	Explanation	Post. Ref.	Debit		Credit		Balance	
							Debit	Credit

Complete this activity.

3.2   **Prepare a trial balance for Kline's Cleaning Service**, using the information from the ledger accounts. The date of the trial balance is the date of the last entry posted to the ledger. NOTE: List all accounts, whether or not they have balances.

ACCOUNT TITLE	ACCT. NO.	DEBIT		CREDIT	

Summary

Posting from the General Journal:

1. Write the date in the date column.
2. Write the journal page number in the Post. Ref. column of the account.
3. Write the amount in the debit or credit column of the proper account.
4. Calculate the new account balance. Enter the new balance in the debit or credit balance column as determined by the account's normal balance.
5. Write the account number in the Post. Ref. column of the journal showing the account to which the item was posted.

Proving Cash:

1. Determine the cash balance on the last check stub.
2. Compare the check stub balance to the cash account balance in the ledger.

Preparing a Trial Balance:

1. Complete the header with *who*, *what*, and *when*.
2. Copy the last balance from the debit or credit balance column of each account in the general ledger.
3. List the account and their balances with debit balances in the first column and credit balances in the second column.
4. Total the debit balances (column one) and the credit balances (column two).
5. Compare to be sure that the debit and credit balances are equal. Remember, in a double-entry system, debits must always equal credits.

Searching for Errors:

1. Re-add the trial balance columns.
2. Make sure no accounts have been omitted. Compare account titles and balances with the general ledger account titles and balances.
3. Re-add each ledger account to determine the accuracy of its balance.
4. Check the posting of each item from the journal to the ledger.
5. Check the equality of the debit and credit in the journal.

Review the material in this section in preparation for the Self Test. This Self Test will check your mastery of this particular section as well as your knowledge of the previous sections.

31

SELF TEST 3

Match the following descriptions with the correct account number (each answer, 2 points).

3.01	_____ first asset account	a. 510
3.02	_____ first expense account	b. 410
3.03	_____ owner's capital account	c. 220
3.04	_____ first revenue account	d. 215
3.05	_____ second liability account	e. 555
3.06	_____ third asset account	f. 110
3.07	_____ fifth expense account	g. 310
3.08	_____ owner's drawing account	h. 210
3.09	_____ first liability account	i. 130
3.010	_____ fifth asset account	j. 320
3.011	_____ a new liability account inserted between the first and second liability accounts	k. 150
		l. 666
3.012	_____ a new expense account inserted between the fifth and sixth expense accounts	m. 550
		n. 125
3.013	_____ a new asset account inserted between the second and third asset accounts	

Determine the current balance of each account based upon the transactions that have been posted from the general journal (each answer, 2 points).

3.014   AN ACCOUNT WITH A NORMAL DEBIT BALANCE:

Date 20—	Explanation	Post. Ref.	Debit	Credit	Balance Debit	Balance Credit
Jan. 1		1	19800 00		19800 00	
3		1		800 00		
7		1	1250 00			
12		1		1565 00		
18		1		2225 00		
28		1	1458 00			
30		1		3568 00		

ACCOUNTING

four

LIFEPAC TEST

$$\frac{139}{174}$$

Name _____

Date _____

Score _____

LIFEPAC TEST ACCOUNTING 4

Complete the following activity.

Robert Burns opened a real estate business called **Burns Realty** which uses the following accounts:

Cash	110
Accounts Receivable	120
Office Supplies	130
Office Equipment	140
Automobile	150
Land	160
Building	170
Accounts Payable	210
Mortgage Payable	220
Robert Burns, Capital	310
Robert Burns, Drawing	320
Appraisal Fees	410
Commissions	420
Advertising Expense	510
Miscellaneous Expense	520
Salaries Expense	530

1. **Open the general ledger accounts** from the chart of accounts given above.

2. **Journalize transactions** in page 1 of a general journal. Source documents are abbreviated as follows: check, **Ck**; Memorandum, **M**; purchase invoice, **P**; receipt, **R**.

3. **Post the journal entries** to the general ledger.

4. **Prepare a trial balance**, using the date of the last journal entry.

Transactions:

April 1 Invested $68,000.00 cash and office equipment with a fair market value of $15,000.00 in a real estate agency, M1

2 Purchased land worth $62,000.00 and a building valued at $110,000.00. Paid $33,000.00 cash and signed a mortgage to pay the balance over 5 years, Ck100

3 Bought office supplies on account, $975.00, P2

4 Purchased an automobile for the business, $17,500.00, Ck101

5 Paid office salaries, $600.00, Ck102

6 Sold a piece of property and was paid $8,900.00 commission, R1

7 Paid $250.00 for advertising in a local trade publication, Ck103

8 Paid $75.00 on account for supplies purchased on April 3, Ck104

9 Bought a new computer on account for the office, $1,840.00, P3

10 Completed an appraisal on account and billed the client $210.00, M2

11 Paid office salaries, $640.00, Ck105

12 Received on account, $210.00 from client billed on April 10, R2

13 Withdrew $1,500.00 for personal use by owner, Ck106

JOURNAL								Page	
Date	Account Title and Explanation	Doc No.	Post. Ref.	General Debit		General Credit			

Account Title:						Account No.	
Date	Explanation	Post. Ref.	Debit	Credit	Balance		
					Debit	Credit	

Account Title:						Account No.	
Date	Explanation	Post. Ref.	Debit	Credit	Balance		
					Debit	Credit	

Account Title:						Account No.	
Date	Explanation	Post. Ref.	Debit	Credit	Balance		
					Debit	Credit	

Account Title:						Account No.	
Date	Explanation	Post. Ref.	Debit	Credit	Balance		
					Debit	Credit	

Account Title:					Account No.			
Date	Explanation	Post. Ref.	Debit		Credit		Balance	
							Debit	Credit

Account Title:					Account No.			
Date	Explanation	Post. Ref.	Debit		Credit		Balance	
							Debit	Credit

Account Title:					Account No.			
Date	Explanation	Post. Ref.	Debit		Credit		Balance	
							Debit	Credit

Account Title:					Account No.			
Date	Explanation	Post. Ref.	Debit		Credit		Balance	
							Debit	Credit

Account Title:					Account No.			
Date	Explanation	Post. Ref.	Debit		Credit		Balance	
							Debit	Credit

Account Title:						Account No.	
Date	Explanation	Post. Ref.	Debit	Credit	Balance		
					Debit	Credit	

Account Title:						Account No.	
Date	Explanation	Post. Ref.	Debit	Credit	Balance		
					Debit	Credit	

Account Title:						Account No.	
Date	Explanation	Post. Ref.	Debit	Credit	Balance		
					Debit	Credit	

Account Title:						Account No.	
Date	Explanation	Post. Ref.	Debit	Credit	Balance		
					Debit	Credit	

Account Title:						Account No.	
Date	Explanation	Post. Ref.	Debit	Credit	Balance		
					Debit	Credit	

Account Title: **Account No.**

Date	Explanation	Post. Ref.	Debit	Credit	Balance	
					Debit	Credit

Account Title: **Account No.**

Date	Explanation	Post. Ref.	Debit	Credit	Balance	
					Debit	Credit

ACCOUNT TITLE	ACCT. NO.	DEBIT	CREDIT

NOTES

AN ACCOUNT WITH A NORMAL CREDIT BALANCE:

Date 20–		Explanation	Post. Ref.	Debit	Credit	Balance Debit	Balance Credit
Jan.	1		1		11800 00		11800 00
	5		1		800 00		
	7		1	1687 00			
	12		1		56 00		
	18		1	8250 00			
	28		1	458 00			
	30		1		5368 00		

For the accounts listed below, indicate the following (each answer, 3 points).

- the proper **account number**,
- the account's **normal balance** (*debit* or *credit*), and
- which report the account would be listed on: **balance sheet** or **income statement**

(NOTE: Remember that assets are listed in order of liquidity and expenses are listed alphabetically.)

3.016

Account Title		Account Number	Balance Side	Balance Sheet or Income Statement
Cash	a.			
Accounts Payable	b.			
Advertising Expense	c.			
Sales	d.			
Petty Cash	e.			
Rent Expense	f.			
Accounts Receivable	g.			
Miscellaneous Expense	h.			
Delivery Equipment	i.			
Salary Expense	j.			
Buildings	k.			
Prepaid Insurance	l.			
Utilities Expense	m.			
John Smith, Capital	n.			
Supplies	o.			
Supplies Expense	p.			

Number the steps of the posting process in their correct order (each answer, 2 points).

3.017 a. _____ Enter the ledger account number in the Post. Ref. column of the journal.

b. _____ Enter the amount of the debit in the debit amount column of the appropriate ledger account.

c. _____ Enter the journal page number in the Post. Ref. column of the account.

d. _____ Add the posted amount to the previous debit balance (if any) and enter the new balance in the debit balance column.

e. _____ Enter the date of the journal entry in the date column of the ledger account.

SECTION IV. REVIEW & APPLICATION PROBLEMS

 Complete the following activities.

Don Levy owns a service business called **Rent-A-Tool**.

4.1 **Open general ledger accounts** based on the chart of accounts shown below for Rent-A-Tool.

RENT-A-TOOL CHART OF ACCOUNTS			
Balance Sheet		**Income Statement**	
Assets		**Revenue**	
Cash	110	Sales	410
Supplies	120		
Prepaid Insurance	130	**Expenses**	
Liabilities		Advertising Expense	510
		Miscellaneous Expense	520
Snapp's Supply	210	Rent Expense	530
Owner's Equity		Repair Expense	540
Don Levy, Capital	310	Utilities Expense	550
Don Levy, Drawing	320		

Post the following journal entries to the ledger accounts you opened.

JOURNAL

Page /

Date 20—		Account Title and Explanation	Doc No.	Post. Ref.	General Debit		General Credit	
May	1	Cash			14500	00		
		Don Levy, Capital	R1				14500	00
	3	Prepaid Insurance			1350	00		
		Cash	Ck 1				1350	00
	5	Supplies			1400	00		
		Snapp's Supply	P1				1400	00
	5	Rent Expense			950	00		
		Cash	Ck 2				950	00
	7	Miscellaneous Expense			5	00		
		Cash	Ck 3				5	00
	8	Supplies			1050	00		
		Cash	Ck 4				1050	00
	8	Cash			1650	00		
		Sales	T8				1650	00
	9	Snapp's Supply			1400	00		
		Cash	Ck 5				1400	00
	10	Repair Expense			85	00		
		Cash	Ck 6				85	00
	11	Advertising Expense			110	00		
		Cash	Ck 7				110	00
	12	Cash			1150	00		
		Sales	T12				1150	00
	14	Utilities Expense			75	00		
		Cash	Ck 8				75	00
	14	Cash			550	00		
		Sales	T14				550	00
	15	Don Levy, Drawing			450	00		
		Cash	Ck 9				450	00
	16	Cash			675	00		
		Sales	T16				675	00

Account Title:

Account No.

Date		Explanation	Post. Ref.	Debit		Credit		Balance			
								Debit		Credit	

Account Title:

Account No.

Date		Explanation	Post. Ref.	Debit		Credit		Balance			
								Debit		Credit	

Account Title:

Account No.

Date		Explanation	Post. Ref.	Debit		Credit		Balance			
								Debit		Credit	

Account Title: _____ Account No. _____

Date	Explanation	Post. Ref.	Debit	Credit	Balance Debit	Balance Credit

Account Title: _____ Account No. _____

Date	Explanation	Post. Ref.	Debit	Credit	Balance Debit	Balance Credit

Account Title: _____ Account No. _____

Date	Explanation	Post. Ref.	Debit	Credit	Balance Debit	Balance Credit

Account Title: _____ Account No. _____

Date	Explanation	Post. Ref.	Debit	Credit	Balance Debit	Balance Credit

Account Title: _____   **Account No.** _____

Date		Explanation	Post. Ref.	Debit	Credit	Balance	
						Debit	Credit

Account Title: _____   **Account No.** _____

Date		Explanation	Post. Ref.	Debit	Credit	Balance	
						Debit	Credit

Account Title: _____   **Account No.** _____

Date		Explanation	Post. Ref.	Debit	Credit	Balance	
						Debit	Credit

Account Title: _____   **Account No.** _____

Date		Explanation	Post. Ref.	Debit	Credit	Balance	
						Debit	Credit

Account Title: _____   **Account No.** _____

Date		Explanation	Post. Ref.	Debit	Credit	Balance	
						Debit	Credit

4.3 **Prove cash**, using the total of the Cash account and the checkbook balance shown on the check stub below.

Cash Account Balance: a. _____

Checkbook Balance: b. _____

Check No.	10		
Date		, 20___	
To			
For			
Balance Forwarded		13050	00
Deposit			

Complete the following activity.

Tammy Jennings owns a pet grooming business called **Pet-A-Care**. The following information is included to complete the necessary records for Pet-A-Care.

Pet-A-Care uses the following accounts:

Cash
Office Max (creditor)
Advertising Expense
Supplies
Salary Expense
Grooming Fees
Prepaid Insurance
West's Grooming Supplies (creditor)
Office Equipment
Miscellaneous Expense
Tammy Jennings, Capital
Rent Expense
Repair Expense
Tammy Jennings, Drawing
Utilities Expense

4.4 **Prepare a chart of accounts for Pet-A-Care** on the form provided below. The chart of accounts is divided according to the two financial reports a business must prepare: the balance sheet and the income statement. Use the example in problem 4.1 if necessary.

4.5 **Open general ledger accounts** for each of the accounts listed on the chart of accounts for Pet-A-Care.

Date 20—		Account Title and Explanation	Doc No.	Post. Ref.	General Debit		General Credit	
June	1	Cash			20000	00		
		Tammy Jennings, Capital	R1				20000	00
	2	Rent Expense			900	00		
		Cash	Ck 1				900	00
	3	Supplies			1600	00		
		Cash	Ck 2				1600	00
	4	Office Equipment			18000	00		
		Office Max	P1				18000	00
	5	Prepaid Insurance			600	00		
		Cash	Ck 3				600	00
	5	Cash			1900	00		
		Grooming Fees	T5				1900	00
	8	Office Max			1200	00		
		Cash	Ck 4				1200	00
	9	Repair Expense			65	00		
		Cash	Ck 5				65	00
	9	Salary Expense			789	00		
		Cash	Ck 6				789	00
	10	Supplies			1300	00		
		West's Grooming Supplies	P2				1300	00
	10	Advertising Expense			75	00		
		Cash	Ck 7				75	00
	11	Tammy Jennings, Drawing			450	00		
		Cash	Ck 8				450	00
	12	Supplies			980	00		
		Cash	Ck 9				980	00

Date 20—		Account Title and Explanation	Doc No.	Post. Ref.	General Debit		General Credit	
June	13	Cash			3450	00		
		Grooming Fees	I13				3450	00
	13	Supplies			850	00		
		West's Grooming Supplies	P3				850	00
	14	Salary Expense			989	00		
		Cash	Ck 10				989	00
	15	Office Max			1200	00		
		Cash	Ck 11				1200	00
	16	Cash			3590	00		
		Grooming Fees	I16				3590	00
	19	West's Grooming Supplies			1300	00		
		Cash	Ck 12				1300	00
	20	Prepaid Insurance			1250	00		
		Cash	Ck 13				1250	00
	22	Advertising Expense			85	00		
		Cash	Ck 14				85	00
	23	Tammy Jennings, Drawing			550	00		
		Cash	Ck 15				550	00
	30	Salary Expense			780	00		
		Cash	Ck 16				780	00
	30	Utilities Expense			656	00		
		Cash	Ck 17				656	00
	30	Miscellaneous Expense			92	00		
		Cash	Ck 18				92	00

4.6 **Post all entries** from the general journal.

Account Title:						Account No.		
Date	Explanation	Post. Ref.	Debit	Credit	Balance			
					Debit		Credit	

Account Title:						Account No.		
Date	Explanation	Post. Ref.	Debit	Credit	Balance			
					Debit		Credit	

Account Title:						Account No.	
Date	Explanation	Post. Ref.	Debit	Credit	Balance		
					Debit	Credit	

Account Title:						Account No.	
Date	Explanation	Post. Ref.	Debit	Credit	Balance		
					Debit	Credit	

Account Title:						Account No.	
Date	Explanation	Post. Ref.	Debit	Credit	Balance		
					Debit	Credit	

Account Title:						Account No.	
Date	Explanation	Post. Ref.	Debit	Credit	Balance		
					Debit	Credit	

Account Title:					Account No.			
Date		Explanation	Post. Ref.	Debit	Credit	Balance		
						Debit		Credit

Account Title:					Account No.			
Date		Explanation	Post. Ref.	Debit	Credit	Balance		
						Debit		Credit

Account Title:					Account No.			
Date		Explanation	Post. Ref.	Debit	Credit	Balance		
						Debit		Credit

Account Title:					Account No.			
Date		Explanation	Post. Ref.	Debit	Credit	Balance		
						Debit		Credit

Account Title: **Account No.**

Date	Explanation	Post. Ref.	Debit	Credit	Balance Debit	Balance Credit

Account Title: **Account No.**

Date	Explanation	Post. Ref.	Debit	Credit	Balance Debit	Balance Credit

Account Title: **Account No.**

Date	Explanation	Post. Ref.	Debit	Credit	Balance Debit	Balance Credit

Account Title: **Account No.**

Date	Explanation	Post. Ref.	Debit	Credit	Balance Debit	Balance Credit

Account Title:						Account No.		
Date		Explanation	Post. Ref.	Debit	Credit	Balance		
						Debit		Credit

4.7   **Prove cash**, using the total of the Cash account and the checkbook balance shown on the check stub below.

        Cash Account Balance: a. _____

        Checkbook Balance: b. _____

Check No.	19	
Date	, 20___	
To		
For		
Balance Forwarded	15379	00
Deposit		

48

4.8   **Prepare a trial balance** for Pet-A-Care on the form provided below.

ACCOUNT TITLE	ACCT. NO.	DEBIT	CREDIT

Complete the following activity.

Wilma Poole owns a jewelry repair shop called **Poole's Gold** which uses the following accounts:

Assets		**Revenue**	
Cash	110	Repair Fees	410
Supplies	120		
Prepaid Insurance	130	**Expenses**	
Office Equipment	140	Advertising Expense	510
		Miscellaneous Expense	520
Liabilities		Rent Expense	530
Gold 'n Things	210	Repair Expense	540
Wilson's Supply	220	Salary Expense	550
		Utilities Expense	560
Capital			
Wilma Poole, Capital	310		
Wilma Poole, Drawing	320		

4.9 **Record the following transactions on page 1** of the general journal. Source documents are abbreviated as follows: check, **Ck**; purchase invoice, **P**; receipt, **R**; calculator tape, **T**.

June 1 Received cash from owner as an additional investment, $4,000.00, R1

2 Paid cash for rent, $1,900.00, Ck1

3 Paid cash for supplies, $1,200.00, Ck2

4 Bought office equipment on account from Wilson's Supply, $1,100.00, P1

5 Paid cash for insurance, $2,600.00, Ck3

5 Received cash for repair fees, $2,980.00, T5

8 Paid cash on account to Wilson's Supply, $1,000.00, Ck4

9 Paid cash for repair, $195.00, Ck5

9 Paid cash for salaries, $1,789.00, Ck6

10 Bought supplies on account from Gold 'n Things, $1,440.00, P2

10 Paid cash for advertising in the local newspaper, $195.00, Ck7

11 Paid cash to owner for personal use, $950.00, Ck8

4.10 **Record the following transactions on page 2** of the general journal.

June 12 Paid cash for postage (Miscellaneous Expense), $80.00, Ck9

13 Received cash for repair fees, $3,950.00, T13

13 Bought supplies on account Wilson's Supply, $1,800.00, P3

14 Paid cash for salaries, $1,789.00, Ck10

15 Paid cash on account to Gold 'n Things, $600.00, Ck11

16 Received cash for repair fees, $2,190.00, T16

20 Paid cash for insurance, $1,410.00, Ck12

22 Paid cash for advertising, $285.00, Ck13

23 Paid the owner for personal use, $650.00, Ck14

30 Paid cash for salaries, $1,789.00, Ck15

30 Paid cash for utilities, $560.00, Ck16

JOURNAL

Page

Date		Account Title and Explanation	Doc No.	Post. Ref.	General Debit		General Credit	

Date	Account Title and Explanation	Doc No.	Post. Ref.	General Debit		General Credit	

JOURNAL

Page

4.11   **Post the general journal items to the ledger.** The ledger accounts have already been opened.

Account Title: *Cash*   **Account No.** *110*

Date 20—		Explanation	Post. Ref.	Debit		Credit		Balance			
								Debit		Credit	
June	1	Opening entry	J1	5000	00			5000	00		

Account Title: *Supplies*   **Account No.** *120*

Date 20—		Explanation	Post. Ref.	Debit		Credit		Balance			
								Debit		Credit	
June	1	Opening entry	J1	600	00			600	00		

Account Title: *Prepaid Insurance* **Account No.** 130

Date 20—		Explanation	Post. Ref.	Debit		Credit		Balance Debit		Credit	
June	1	Opening entry	J1	800	00			800	00		

Account Title: *Office Equipment* **Account No.** 140

Date 20—		Explanation	Post. Ref.	Debit		Credit		Balance Debit		Credit	
June	1	Opening entry	J1	6000	00			6000	00		

Account Title: *Gold 'n Things* **Account No.** 210

Date 20—		Explanation	Post. Ref.	Debit		Credit		Balance Debit		Credit	
June	1	Opening entry	J1			600	00			600	00

Account Title: *Wilson's Supply* **Account No.** 220

Date 20—		Explanation	Post. Ref.	Debit		Credit		Balance Debit		Credit	
June	1	Opening entry	J1			2000	00			2000	00

Account Title: Wilma Poole, Capital   Account No. 310

Date 20—		Explanation	Post. Ref.	Debit		Credit		Balance Debit		Balance Credit	
June	1	Opening entry	J1			9800	00			9800	00

Account Title: Wilma Poole, Drawing   Account No. 320

Date 20—		Explanation	Post. Ref.	Debit		Credit		Balance Debit		Balance Credit	

Account Title: Repair Fees   Account No. 410

Date 20—		Explanation	Post. Ref.	Debit		Credit		Balance Debit		Balance Credit	

Account Title: Advertising Expense   Account No. 510

Date 20—		Explanation	Post. Ref.	Debit		Credit		Balance Debit		Balance Credit	

Account Title: *Miscellaneous Expense*   Account No. *520*

Date 20—		Explanation	Post. Ref.	Debit	Credit	Balance Debit	Balance Credit

Account Title: *Rent Expense*   Account No. *530*

Date 20—		Explanation	Post. Ref.	Debit	Credit	Balance Debit	Balance Credit

Account Title: *Repair Expense*   Account No. *540*

Date 20—		Explanation	Post. Ref.	Debit	Credit	Balance Debit	Balance Credit

Account Title: *Salary Expense*   Account No. *550*

Date 20—		Explanation	Post. Ref.	Debit	Credit	Balance Debit	Balance Credit

Account Title: _Utilities Expense_						Account No. _560_	

Date 20—	Explanation	Post. Ref.	Debit	Credit	Balance Debit	Balance Credit

4.12 **Prepare a trial balance for Poole's Gold.** The date of the last transaction posted to the ledger was June 30th.

ACCOUNT TITLE	ACCT. NO.	DEBIT	CREDIT

OPTIONAL EXERCISES FOR EXTRA CREDIT

 Complete the following activity (153 points).

James Carlson operates a computer repair business, called Carlson's Computer Service which uses the following accounts:

Assets:		Liabilities:		Expenses:	
Cash	110	Accounts Payable	210	Advertising Expense	510
Office Supplies	120	Mortgage Payable	220	Miscellaneous Expense	520
Office Equipment	130	**Capital:**		Rent Expense	530
Repair Equipment	140	James Carlson, Capital	310	Salary Expense	540
Delivery Truck	150	James Carlson, Drawing	320	Utilities Expense	550
Building	160	**Revenue:**			
Land	170	Service Fees	410		

1. **Open the general ledger** for Carlson's Computer Service.

2. **Enter the following balances in the general ledger.**

   Since Carlson's Computer Service is an established business and has already set up ledger accounts, the balances of the permanent accounts (assets, liabilities, and capital) are brought forward from March to April. **To bring the balance forward**, enter the date, the words "Balance Brought Forward," a check mark (✔) in the Post. Ref. column, and the balance in the debit or credit balance column of the account.

Cash	50,000.00	James Carlson, Capital	117,200.00
Office Supplies	1,200.00		
Repair Equipment	6,000.00		
Land	60,000.00		

3. **Record these transactions** on **page 5** of the general journal:

Transactions:

April 1   Mr. Carlson gave his personal office equipment with a fair market value of $18,000.00 to his computer service business, Carlson's Computer Service, M1

     2   Mr. Carlson contracted to have a small office building built for $85,000.00, paying $17,000.00 cash and signing a mortgage to pay the balance over 10 years, Ck100

     3   Bought office supplies on account, $75.00, P2

     4   Purchased a delivery truck for the business, $7,500.00, Ck101

     5   Paid office salaries, $500.00, Ck102

     6   Received $9,200 for computer repair services for the week, T6

     7   Paid $250 for advertising in a local trade publication, Ck103

     8   Paid $75.00 on account for supplies purchased on April 3, Ck104

     9   Bought a new diagnostic computer analyzer on account for the business, $840.00, P3

    10   Paid the rent for April $1,200.00, Ck105

4. **Post** the general journal entries to the ledger.

5. **Prepare a trial balance** for Carlson's Computer Service. Date it the day of the last transaction posted to the ledger. List ALL accounts, even if they do not have balances.

JOURNAL

Date		Account Title and Explanation	Doc No.	Post. Ref.	General Debit		General Credit	

Account Title:						Account No.		
Date		Explanation	Post. Ref.	Debit	Credit	Balance		
						Debit		Credit

Account Title:						Account No.		
Date		Explanation	Post. Ref.	Debit	Credit	Balance		
						Debit		Credit

Account Title:						Account No.		
Date		Explanation	Post. Ref.	Debit	Credit	Balance		
						Debit		Credit

Account Title:						Account No.		
Date		Explanation	Post. Ref.	Debit	Credit	Balance		
						Debit		Credit

60

Account Title:					Account No.		
Date	Explanation	Post. Ref.	Debit	Credit	Balance		
					Debit	Credit	

Account Title:					Account No.		
Date	Explanation	Post. Ref.	Debit	Credit	Balance		
					Debit	Credit	

Account Title:					Account No.		
Date	Explanation	Post. Ref.	Debit	Credit	Balance		
					Debit	Credit	

Account Title:					Account No.		
Date	Explanation	Post. Ref.	Debit	Credit	Balance		
					Debit	Credit	

Account Title:					Account No.		
Date	Explanation	Post. Ref.	Debit	Credit	Balance		
					Debit	Credit	

Account Title:						Account No.	
Date	Explanation	Post. Ref.	Debit	Credit	Balance		
					Debit	Credit	

Account Title:						Account No.	
Date	Explanation	Post. Ref.	Debit	Credit	Balance		
					Debit	Credit	

Account Title:						Account No.	
Date	Explanation	Post. Ref.	Debit	Credit	Balance		
					Debit	Credit	

Account Title:						Account No.	
Date	Explanation	Post. Ref.	Debit	Credit	Balance		
					Debit	Credit	

Account Title:						Account No.	
Date	Explanation	Post. Ref.	Debit	Credit	Balance		
					Debit	Credit	

Account Title:						Account No.		
Date	Explanation	Post. Ref.	Debit	Credit	Balance		
					Debit		Credit	

Account Title:						Account No.		
Date	Explanation	Post. Ref.	Debit	Credit	Balance		
					Debit		Credit	

Account Title:						Account No.		
Date	Explanation	Post. Ref.	Debit	Credit	Balance		
					Debit		Credit	

ACCOUNT TITLE	ACCT. NO.	DEBIT		CREDIT	

Extra forms:

JOURNAL						Page	
Date	Account Title and Explanation	Doc No.	Post. Ref.	General Debit		General Credit	

Extra forms:

ACCOUNT TITLE	ACCT. NO.	DEBIT		CREDIT	